SNAKE
in the
PARSONAGE

SNAKE
in the
PARSONAGE

Award-winning poetry
by Jean Janzen

Intercourse, PA 17534

The author wishes to give grateful acknowledgment to the editors of the following periodicals, in which some of these poems first appeared:

Burning Light, Christianity & Literature, The Cincinnati Poetry Review, The Gettysburg Review, Image, The Journal, Mennonite Life, Poetry ("Gardens of the Body," "Identifying the Fire," "St. Basil's Cathedral," "Toward the End of the Century"), *Potpourri, Prairie Schooner, Quarry West, The Rolling Coulter, South Coast Poetry Journal, West Branch,* and *Yankee.*

"Facets" was published in *The Roberts Writing Awards,* 1990. "Among Orange Trees" was published (in an earlier version) in *National Poetry Competition Winners, 1992,* by the Chester H. Jones Foundation.

Cover photo: Face on a grave in an abandoned Mennonite cemetery in the author's ancestral Polish village.

Cover photograph by Louis Janzen.

Design by Dawn J. Ranck

SNAKE IN THE PARSONAGE
Copyright ©1995 by Jean Janzen
International Standard Book Number: 1-56148-177-7
Library of Congress Catalog Card Number: 95-19505

Library of Congress Cataloging-in-Publication Data

Janzen, Jean.
        Snake in the parsonage : award-winning poetry / by Jean Janzen.
              p. cm.
        ISBN 1-56148-177-7
        I. Title.
        PS3560.A5364S64   1995
        811'.54--dc20   95-19505
                                                                          CIP

for Louis

TABLE OF CONTENTS

PIANO LESSON

Even before she touches the keys,
she can feel it waiting for her
like the rise of foothills,
hills that look softly at her,
that watch her arrive.
The music will demand it,
will draw her into the lovely ache
of suspension, and the slow
dissolving into harmony, again and again.
She is so young, she cannot understand.
Yet somehow she knows
it is inevitable, and with a sigh
she opens the book and begins.

I.

Identifying
the Fire

IDENTIFYING THE FIRE

Sometimes at night it blooms
in our heads like marigolds
and cockscomb in the cooling garden,

a flare at the end of a long lane
where the ruts finally meet.
Lovers' Lane where my sister and I

carried our dolls, covering
their faces. Lips like fire,
someone said, and we felt a rope

sizzling inside. Our Sunday school teacher
said it was the Holy Ghost hovering,
beating its wings over us

so that every body cell would glow.
All our years a fire consuming,
giving itself away.

We pass it on to our children,
our voices full of love and warnings,
like our own mothers bringing

mustard and tea in the feverish dark,
their hands both soothing and electric.
Even in old age they cradle

a burning as they lean
over pots of geraniums and break off
the stems to help them bloom.

All night the petals scatter
over them, and they stir as though
toward another, someone who once

entered them. A time out of time
kindling the next breath,
and at its far end, branches, gesturing.

AT DRAKE'S BAY

God wanted you to be, my mother tells me.
Six children and the doctor offering
little advice. And yet, choices.
My grandmother ends her life
and my father is adrift. At fourteen
he washes onto the prairies of Canada.
She had stared for days, her children
begging her to speak. It is April,
the earth's first green blazing
under the pull of the Ukrainian sky
which shatters over her,
smothering her. And the children
scatter like pebbles.

What corridors of water and wind
brought me to life?
My mother, eighty now, stands with me
on these scoured stones where Drake
blew in, down to his last vessel.
The doctor suggested abstinence,
she laughs. And we laugh together.
The bright wind whips our bodies
and roars in our ears,
the blue mussels in thick colonies
cling under the surge of the breakers.

NEW COUNTRY

We entered, all nine of us,
by way of Portal, North Dakota,
into the USA. June 14, 1939,
and the flags all out.
The stripes snapped overhead
and the screen door of the Five and Dime
slammed in the rising wind.
Then the storm emptied over us
as we drove south, our Chevy
weaving in mud like a slow boat.
I could hardly see our new country
to which God had sent us—
the rain's brown slosh and all of us
breathing the windows into a blur.
And when we entered the small Minnesota town,
it was night, the bandstand hunched
under black dripping trees, the flags
folded away, and no one around.
No one to say, *This now is yours.*
Only the frogs' relentless calls
to a distant rumbling.
But before summer was out
I had memorized the pledge of allegiance
and once rose from my bed
in my sleep to recite it.
My sisters raised their heads
from their pillows, startled
by my small, speaking figure,
hand over my heart, giving myself
to whatever would have me—
the window, the wet breeze, the stars
as they drowned in the growing light of day.

SUMMER IN THE DARK: 1944

1

In church, men on one side,
women on the other. That summer
the men argued over God's will
and a new roof as we sat perspiring
in the pews, barely breathing.
And when Anna Wiens died, age 14
and unbaptized because of the feud,
we all stared at her in the summer light,
her auburn hair and freckles scattered
over the starched white pillow.
                    Sometimes in the long light
of July my father took me with him
to the Altenheim with its odors
of Lysol and borscht, and the stroke victim
near the nurse's desk, his mouth open
in a perpetual silent scream. And up
the wooden stairs, a roomful of women
softening in their chairs as evening arrived
through spotless windows. My father
pressed their hands whispering *Gnade*
and *Ewigkeit* as I stood by. Then the car
hunching forward in the dark, silence
all the way home.

2

After harvest we visited the CPS boys
in the alternate service camps.
Some worked the saws, some were paratroopers
fighting fires. And some would run their hands
along my braids, ask about school.
"Flirt," my sister called me.

My heart beat fast in the filled mess hall,
and for one bright evening I knew
these men could save me, even without guns.
Someone from this room would come
to my rescue, maybe drop softly from the sky
and take me in his arms, away from the drone
and the fire.
                    Yet in the blackouts,
the prayers over and over. For in that warm
darkness, all I could see were two paths:
everlasting punishment and everlasting joy.
And at the road's black fork, Miss Lepp's
stern white face, her hip bone jutting out,
her finger in my eye. All summer, her face
and the wind rasping through the cornfield,
bending the cottonwoods by the creek.
And every night the maple scraped the windowscreen,
its arms gesticulating, beckoning, as if
it wanted everything from me, wanted me—
my eyes dry and open hour after hour, wanted
the quick hammering of my heart. Everything.
Even the darkness which I clutched
in my hands when I prayed.

FACETS

All the way from the Nickel-Back Cafe
past the college to home,
the block of ice shimmers
in its growing puddle.
The wagon wheels stir up the hot dust
of September. Now father slides it
into the icebox. Thud of the door,
sighs as he leans once more over the Doctrine
of Christ and the required genetics.
Fifty, already gray, he has brought us
on his journey of learning.
To know the truth, to hold it up
and examine it, like sun on crystal.
This is the year I turn thirteen,
the year of my catechism:
What are the attributes of God,
the five steps to salvation?
The sun spins over the men's dorm
where we live, scorches the elms,
clamors against the windowpanes.
At night cicadas drill their urgencies
and the college men shout and gallop
on the stairs. I can hardly hear
my own heart, its din of voices calling
to my father to rescue me
from the baptismal waters.
In the shadowed kitchen he is bending
over books, and drop by drop the ice
redefines itself in the dark.

ANNA RIEGER AT THE BLACKBOARD

As her stickmen warred
on the chalk-green hills,
her body swayed from army to army.

Gideon blew his trumpet
and with one swish of the eraser,
thousands fell, and her crepe dress

shivered. Her blue chalk
in a side-swoop taught us grace,
Moses' water cascading

out of a rock-struck-right.
Once in the girls' room,
we found her bent over,

brushing her hair, all tumbled
now out of its bun.
When she lifted herself up

to the mirror, her face
was flushed and strong.
Her comb held high,

she parted the brown silk and caught
it again, pushed the door open
with one full hip, and entered

the crowded halls. And we followed,
girls and boys, as on both sides
the sea walls stood
clear and bright and quivering.

NOTE TO DEE

Today I almost bought a canary
in memory of your mother,
her basement full of yellow feathers
and song. I wonder now
at her comfort with disorder,
the brilliant fabrics strewn about
in the dining room for your sisters'
elegant dresses, her garden
a riot of mulberries and roses.
                    When you and I
lay floating on blooming flax fields,
our inland ocean, we saw only
the clean arc of sky and imagined
our full and orderly futures.
Lying there, looking up,
we didn't see the horizon
which your mother anxiously scanned
before harvest. We floated freely
among the spokes of light, tunes
smoldering in our chests.
                    You wrote
that at the end her once-tall frame
diminished and curled; the barn
is gone, apple trees cut.
What is left is her laughter, the way
she laughed when we ran through
the open door and into her arms,
wet and windblown from the storm.
Even as the thunder tried to swallow it,
here it is, clearly hers, falling now
like pearls into my lap, luminous
and rolling, gathered
from the chaos of the sea.

SNAKE IN THE PARSONAGE

I found it in the cellar,
sleek and curled around
empty Mason jars when I went down
for pickled beets, cried for my father
to come with a shovel.
This parsonage an ongoing irritation
for my mother, a square white house
in the middle of the barren plain.
All year, a strong wind
driving grit through every crack,
the steep, narrow stairs,
the laundry lines strung
beside the gravel road.
All of it planned wrong, she said,
rinsing the sheets once more.
As if we were reading the Bible
backwards, this four-square manse
set down like the holy city
of Revelation an eternity ago,
reversing its stories of miracle
and its weeping prophets.
And now we were back to the beginning,
one family in a desert
with a serpent, even before
the Garden, when creation
had barely begun. Nothing
on the horizon of this flat land
except the setting sun, evening
after evening, so brilliant
in its fuchsias and golds,
everything waiting to begin.

CHICKEN GUTS

After the sticky steam of plums
and the fuzz of peaches, we caught chickens
in the yard, stewing hens for canning.
Dad with a hatchet on the old elm stump
and I in the cellar scraping grit out of gizzards.
All in a sort of ritual dance: the chop,
the boiling body-dip for defeathering, the swing
through the singe of fire. Then, disembowel, dismember.
All for the grand finale behind glass—a chorus line
of chicken legs caught in the kick, like a photo.
This is not about death, or violence to animals,
not even about sex. It's about those intestines
I stripped into the bucket. About how they
could have been saved, stretched across a hollow,
and made to sing. It's about my cousin Eugene
who plucks and saws the gut of his cello until
something throbs in our own. And it's about dance,
not the scratch and kick of the chicken's life,
but the deep stomp that awakens the bottom
of the lake, the dance I want to do among
the festival of wild grass and flowers back
in my hometown. I want to lean low,
to paint my face with mulberry juice
and stay up all night. I want to put my ear
against the belly of the earth to hear
it rumble, to hear it sigh.

II.

Looking
for the Soul

DIVIDING THE NIGHT

All night the bells of Westkirche
clang their quarter hours.
The pitches are off and homey

like a kitchen clock emptying
into the shadows, mother clattering
plates and silver while father naps

beneath the mantel clock, the one
he takes down once a year
to boil the inner parts.

"It's silence that awakens you,"
he said, his eyes suddenly
flying open. As now this silence

cuts in, surgical, a vertical slice
into the old flow of gears
clicking softly, of brass weights

pulling down. Not the silence
of hunger or waiting, but a sudden truth
after sound, after each part

has done its work, winding and loosening.
After we try words and fail, spilling
out like love, then stop.

And there it is, simple as an empty
chair, the cleared table,
the kitchen light filling the room.

ORDER

Saturday afternoon, father in his study
hunts and pecks the Order of Service.
I can still see it, the invocation,
hymn of praise, the growing columns of words.
Rock and fortress, he will say tomorrow,
wings over us. And set on a table
between the pillars is his sermon,
a pitcherful shivering until morning.
Keys clatter, the return bar swings down
to the benediction, his arms over the people.
They will stand like these inked letters,
surrounded by silence, a whiteness
that vibrates like the ceiling in his study,
which sometimes rises and opens, books
towering on all sides—*My Utmost for His Highest,
The Cloud of Unknowing*—the pages
like slippery steps, and forever turning.

WOMEN OF THE CLOTH

1

My mother sings "Rescue the Perishing"
as she quilts with the others,
her stitches are deep and quick
into the ocean waves which vibrate
orange and green, barely contained
in the purple border.
She has snipped hundreds of triangles,
then joined them with her treadle machine,
her small feet pumping into high speed.
Jesus, Jesus, she sings into her rapid
stitches. Jesus naked in the barn,
bruised on the windy hills,
the women wrapping him in cloths.
And yet he escapes like light,
vibrating through the prism
of the story, faster
than her eye can follow.

2

Emma Yoder measures each corner
carefully, takes her time.
The kingdom comes inch by inch
like the *"Lobsang"* with its fourteen
verses, its long, embroidered notes.
Oh, how these colors praise him,
the bars pulsing their blue
against the red of cranberries.
She must break perfection with one piece;
she will make it yellow, startling,
the color of God's eye burning
among the wheat shocks,
his flame licking the stubble
until the whole field glows.
Broad as her husband's shoulders
approaching her in lamplight—
what no fence can contain.

3

As a child I heard it in music,
saw it in the sky, something
offering itself, reaching out.
Sometimes in the beauty of fabric,
bolts and bolts of extravagant colors,
the plush of velvet.
Once, from a remnant, my mother
made me an ivory satin blouse.
All season in church
I stroked it as I sang,
smooth as sky, or my heart,
which I must open for Jesus
to come in, the blood flaring out
like a rose. Then he would unfurl
the white percale, the preacher said,
so I could walk the long road.
Trying not to leave a single stain,
I will walk until I die,
when I will sprout wings.
I will never have to touch
the earth again.

GOING WEST

I think how young my father was
when he followed the sun half-way
around the world, the sea carrying him.
Then on Sunday afternoons he sat alone
on his attic bed and cried, not for home,
but for lack of it. But when I knew him,
he held my mother on his lap, stroked
her and murmured, you are my home, knowing
she could slip away like molten gold.
                       I see the sun
drop its forge into the Pacific,
the gilded waves turn back to steel.
I think of ancestors staring out
over the Baltic, that pure northern light
beckoning me. Somewhere, beyond
the water, a place we glimpse
in prayers, in sexual ecstasy, in pain.
On every shore the water asking,
fire or ice, what do you want,
opening its arms.

HOW THEY LOVED

Inside each of us lies the secret
of our parents. We carry it

like a small stone buried
and glimmering—how they loved

under the layered pressures
and the scouring of days, the stream

singing over them. Hidden.
But sometimes we catch a glimpse

inside a darkened room where a pair
of glassblowers work beside the furnace-

glow. They shape a vessel
with their breaths, the dance

of their bodies, and the firing.
They hold it up to the lamp,

turning it. "See how strong," they say,
and test it on the old brick floor

where it rolls, whole, in that other
country we hold inside of us, where some days

they stroll together in a city square,
bright with mist under the sliding sun.

AMONG ORANGE TREES

Today in the orange grove across the street,
a man parked his car and pounded his fists
into a woman. She sat swollen with her unborn,
guarding her face and belly in a jerking dance.
The March grass stood green around them
and the sun was high. What had he lost
in this fertile season, falling and rotten in the furrows?

All afternoon the trees glowed boldly in their satin leaves,
and I wondered how tenderness is born and kept.
I remembered my father caressing my mother,
his calm responses to trouble. How once
someone paid his way to California, and when we met him
at the train depot, he reached into his satchel
for a small bottle of cologne which I have kept
unopened to this day. *From the crushed orange blossoms,*
he said, as he opened my hand and put it there.

IN THE MISSION GARDEN

Hummingbirds twit in the larkspur,
jet from hibiscus to lily and into
the pepper trees. They claim this space

as Father Serra once did, and the Indians
before him, when they wore only mud
and patches of rabbit skin.

Serra, who "gathered their souls,"
dressed them in white for baptism,
filed them into this courtyard

under the spinning flights of birds and sun.
The soul cries for order, he said,
begs to be clothed in purity,

to receive respite from the frenzy
of hungers. But the immense sky
was over him, the birds flashed jewels

and the bougainvillea thronged
with fuchsia and nectar. The young students
sang with aching sweetness, their skin

shining and succulent. He wanted to gather
it all and keep it, not be purified
into nothingness. He wanted

to be full, holding everything,
condensed, yet nearly weightless,
so he could arch and hover,

so he could skim the currents
and the wheels of the sun.

TOWARD THE END OF THE CENTURY

Worst is the ivy
    which works its way
through a window crack when
    I turn my head, then pushes
a pale arm through the drapery.
    Good, proper English ivy
turned to forced entry.
    But also, the creeping fig,
at first so demure,
    has grown hungry and large,
etches the brick and window glass
    with a million hands.
I open the door for air
    and the moths swarm in.
One night a baby possum
    at the doorstep, one paw up, courteous.
Even after the garden shears
    and the locked doors, honeybees
continue to claim the chimney,
    generation after generation
filling it with their tiny rooms,
    snarling angrily when we try
to gas them out.
    And when I play Chopin's Prelude in A Flat
some fly in to the sudden sun
    of the piano light, scorching
their wings as I repeat
    the one essential tone,
the search for resolution.

SLEEPLESS UNDER DOWN

Every morning Maria fluffs
my down pillow and drapes it
with lace, Russian style.
It is a container for grief
and for love, for the memory
of her mother stripping the breasts
of geese. Her browned hands
would grasp and release in quick
motion as she sat, placid,
among the racket of feathers.
During the war Maria dreamed
that the geese clamored over
her bed with burning wings,
moaning with hunger. Then, all day
she stood at the window hugging
her mother's dress until her gray figure
approached in the dark, home at last
from the barns of bawling cattle.
And under her skirt, two dead rats
she had trapped for supper.
When father finally staggered home
from the camps, mother patched his rags
with every color. Like Joseph,
she says, his ankles thin in the fields.
Now I lie sleepless under
a softness that was lost and saved,
that once grew lean and desperate enough
to lift its wings into the night.

ST. BASIL'S CATHEDRAL

These nine domes
are wrapped chocolates,
rings, a striped silk shirt,

an amaryllis bud bulging
into the world, all crammed
over thick walls, its base

entwined with painted vines
and roses. Narrow passageways
lead to intimate chapels

lined with kissed icons,
each room a lacquered box,
a treasury of earth's colors

open and offered:
the robes of velvet hills,
limestone hands uncovering

the heart, golden ash leaves
flung up into wings.
And above it all,

the ceiling rises
to a dizzying swirl of mosaic
blues. Such light,

it ignites everything—
cheeks of the saints,
the slope of their shoulders,
Mary's eyes, black as coal.

FINDING THE PEARL

They burned the body parts for days,
pouring acid on the stubborn bones, dropping
the ashes into a mine shaft. Even then,
the old tutor, weeping, found evidence,
the Czarina's pearl earring,
one of a pair she always wore.
In 1916 her hand swerves the path of our century
as she writes her letters—the Czar fires
one statesman after another while their son
writhes in his bed, the blood spreading undetected.
Pearl in the tutor's hand,
the nacre which hardened into layers
of death, the sky of Siberia iridescent
over the vast fields of bones.
And the fire in the pit still burns.

I think of her when I see Vermeer's women
in the daylight of their rooms, pearls gleaming
on their ears and held in their hands.
After a lifetime of painting, his brush
made their faces more luminous,
the layers of years building into
such light. Like the pearl of great price—
you sell everything to get it, the Gospel says,
then hold it loose in your hand.
Not the clutching loves of nation, child
or even God, but a beauty that gives itself away.
You walk the museum galleries gazing
at the treasures, then turn another corner
and there it is, the face you didn't know
you were looking for, open as light,
its fires and its tides.

HOME

Sometimes while cleaning the house,
I raise my feather duster high
and do a Slavic stomp and twirl.
My blue eyes flash in the mirror

as dust flies up
and settles down again.
Sometimes, singing,
I stand in the kitchen sunlight

and break twelve eggs into a bowl
for *paskha,* to eat after Black Saturday,
a tower of yolks, sugar and flour
shaped by fire and air.

Father, when a boy, gaped
at the procession of candles
and the blackened face of the icon.
Then the dance in the village street.

Dust flew around the dizzying skirts,
men stomped and shouted,
and he ran home breathless,
the wind on his bare feet.

Somewhere near Karkhoff
where his mother waited. Home,
now a black ash washed into
the earth, where the wind

moans, where the bones
of his parents wait.
Everything waiting,
bread, dust, the elements of fire,

waiting for the final restoration,
all of us dancing home.

GLOCKEN

We would step from the kitchen's steamy clatter
into the wide silence of winter, its muffle
and glare, and the sled's hushed glide.
When I lay on my back to make an angel,
I didn't think of the frozen dead
or what they couldn't say. But later
when father tipped piled tubs of snow
into the black cistern under the floor,
I heard the echoing plunk, plunk
of what lay beneath us.

Something waits to stir,
to make its dark music. My own voice
caught in the winter fields longs
for the word, clear and running free.
Like the voice of my three year old son
in a febrile seizure. The tense, silent
drive to the hospital, my lift of his slack
body into the December air, and he began
to sing, "Kling, Glocken, kling-a-ling-a-ling"
in a voice high and clear, a bell
in a language he didn't know.

LOOKING FOR THE SOUL

Sometimes in an August night
you think you smell it
in the arbor hanging fragrant

with concords and muscats,
their clusters pulling
at the moon's rising smile.

And you think the soul is weight,
a sweet ripeness that grieves.
What a woman holds in her lap.

Once it was light as a dime,
silver in its slippage
in the sky's arc, or the curved road

of a girl's body. Glide
and drop, of blood, of infant.
Then, of everything.

*

Marble moon, high and riding.
Moon without arms.
As though soul is both weight and drift,

the knife saving it with its cleaving—
baskets heaped with Thompsons and Lady Fingers,
and the vines lifting to the night.

Grass seeds floating, reckless,
on any current. And yet they fall
to the dark foundations

where all is damp with flow
and murmur at the roots, where doors
are open and waiting.

*

Two things will last forever:
this insistence to save what is drifting,
and the need to let it go.

On the arbor, the vines thicken and lean
toward their own collapse,
and the moon blurs

into the western sky, yellowing,
sinking back to earth.
It is a waning crescent

riding on its back,
looking for a place to lie down.
All the empty vaults of night

and still it seeks a room,
a place to lie down inside me.

III.

New Order

DUSTY MILLER MOTH

You came like a dusty miller
into my mother's spotless kitchen
and with your soft wings

circled the light of me.
You came like a cloud
of dusty millers, crowding

with velvet sheddings
among swung brooms, scorching
against the star of my body.

And when the door opened wide,
you filled all my rooms
so that the dark grew pale

with flutterings and we lay,
husked and floating
in the stream that turns

the night-wheel, that grinds
the ripe and gathered grains
of the heavens.

CHICAGO 1954

"So glad you are safe and cared for now,"
my father writes to me, newlywed
and in Chicago, his black script
leaning away. We laugh and I fold
the letter as the El scrapes along
the backbone of the Southside
where we live. Bullet holes in the glass
of our front door, our tires slashed,
and then the pharmacist murdered
at the corner. Almost lakefront,
this neighborhood, yet nothing
but pavement and rocks at the end of 47th
where the water laps and batters.
Lake and wind, a wild pair shining
and cutting by turns, the wind riding
the sooty wing of the steel mills,
then scouring the sky with its next breath.
"Life, it swallows you," the butcher
announces, waving his knife, then handing us
a bologna wafer to taste as we leave
into the rot and ice of the street.

"Breathe in and out," you tell the child,
and listen through your stethoscope
for the sweet exchange of air.
And I lean over a typewriter printing words
under the heart's T-waves. In the evenings
our lips and hands search for that current
that could carry us above the sirens

of the street. But even there, death's face
asking for love. "There is no safety,"
I could have written my father, but he knew that,
knew the howling winds, and the way water rushes
into the ears. "It's underwater where you learn
to trust God," he would say. "You hold your breath
and body against its cold blade," as now I listen
for your familiar footsteps after the long
alley, the opening and closing of three doors,
the turning of your key.

ANNIVERSARIES, JULY 2

Sometimes the fireworks
begin early, on the day
we gave up our independence,

and even on the Fourth
we claim the lights which burst
everywhere as men crouch

with matches on green lawns
and the stadium quivers with booms.
Sometimes the great flowers double

over a body of water;
their petals ride the night
in swooping, hissing arcs,

then enter the dark mirror.
But once on a small peninsula
high over the bay, when crowds

and cars jammed the road
for a view, someone threw firecrackers
into the tall, dry grass,

one after another, heedless,
with only two ways to escape:
the black surf far below,

or the one narrow tunnel
toward which we ran, hand in hand,
its entrance already hazy with smoke.

"MOVEMENT OF VAULTED CHAMBERS"

(watercolor by Paul Klee)

Among the crowded,
upright columns
are two that lean.

They form an arch
where nothing is still.
The cut, piled stones

vibrate against
each other in bright
orange and blue.

Stones, I said,
and yet, translucent.
Sections of sheerness

that could fold
and fall,
but are held,

even as foundations
shift, as the purple
sun rolls,

and the hills
slide up
to the moon.

YOU TALK WITH YOUR HANDS

You talk with your hands
       as if the shapes of the alphabet
            need tracing, move each phrase

like a character on your stage of the air.
       But when you stroke my familiar body,
            you speak without sound,

your tactile sentences searching
       for a language lost—a labyrinth we enter
            together, again and again.

We come out clutching and gasping
       for breath, so close were we
            to the original word for union.

And then we lie exhausted, your hands
       motionless now, except for a caress, light
            as the air we divide when we wave goodbye.

A STORY OF LEAVE

(Leave: from the root words *love*
and *belief,* originally *lief*)

First, a man asks permission,
as in "by your leave,"
his hand stretching out.

*

Smooth, as in "Albumblatt,"
much to be desired, Schumann
says, the music pressing
its soft lips,

*

and we turn
in the wind.

*

Liefing: transpiration,
a diet of light.

*

Lobe of my lung,

*

blade,

*

floating.

*

"Don't leave," we say
to each other,
bare-armed, shivering.

NEW ORDER

Under the quilted Love Rings
   we love and cling, all the staggered corners
     of Drunkard's Path meeting over us

in rearrangement. The rings vibrate outward
   as though our drinking of each other
     could make a new order.

And then we sleep, drifting separately
   toward lands we have never seen before.
     Sometimes a bright shore

where quilters toss their needles up
   among the stars, and all the loosened layers
     float. New patterns, colors side by side

we hadn't imagined, even when the warm flush
   of each other rushes through us.
     But sometimes we glimpse it,

awake, what we stumble toward when we leave
   the smoky tavern and let the chill air
     carry us into the brilliance of night.

THE JEWISH BRIDE

Near the end of his life,
Rembrandt saw light coming
more and more from within his sitters,

and so the impasto grows thicker
with reds and yellows which he overbrushed
with a glimmering oil.

The groom's hands hold
his bride's shoulder and breast
lightly, as one would hold light.

They stand among the umber shadows,
the bride bewildered by her bright hands—
and his—the way Rembrandt's wet brush

is stroking gold upon gold
until their bodies flood the canvas
and the whole room where it is hung.

THE ROWING

The morning already full
of a gold-blue glory,
and the wedding party sings its way
to the cliff's edge.
Bride and groom descend the steps
to the beach where a rowboat
waits—his strong thighs,
her veil drifting as he lifts her in.
And then the small vessel
against the wide and shimmering world.

This was years ago.
There was a larger boat
farther out for the honeymoon.
But what I remember was the rowing,
how they leaned and dipped
to the songs from the shore,
how slowly they progressed,
how they are still on their way.

IV.

Wild Grapes

ANOTHER LIFE

According to the broken life-line
in my palm, I should have died by now.
But if you look carefully, you would see
a fine connecting line, like a fresh start.

I think of the breaks that have healed,
the bone's new joining, the skin's
tough, smooth seam. And of my friend Gloria
with the harelip, the soft consonants
of her fifth grade wisdom as she points
to my belly: there is the line where
the doctor cuts for the baby. Gloria, adopted,
who ran away, the wind in her open wounds.

Sometimes only rupture allows breath—
the intubation, the slit of childbirth.
But what of the palsied newborn, or
the friend who emerges without speech?
When endurance is only a dangling thread?

I open my palms and see how they hold
nothing but air, my lifeline.
Survival as light as that. The gratitude
for each breath, its tenacity, how I cling
as it swings me to the other side.

COVER ME

1

You tried to cover us as best you could,
preacher's kids, in dresses from the finest
thrift clothes, quickest sewing pedal in town.
Didn't listen to warnings about pride.
Your eyes burned as you ripped the old seams,
my bright dresses a flare against
the stinginess of the church. Dad's calm reminders
like water on your tongue, and we survived
by the elements. Our crackerbox house
barely covered the ten of us. Who knows
how a mother's spirit holds off danger?
The tornado hit after we moved out.
Stripped off my clothes and knocked me
against a wall, the next owner said.

2

When I offered to wash dishes after supper
you sent me to practice the piano.
I wonder now whether you wanted the music
to take me to places you had never seen,
playing Mozart and Rachmaninoff in the scents
of my first cologne from my first boy,
your hand waving me off into danger.
You knew that my dresses moved like water
when I walked, or was it fire, our true covering?
The way you now let your good dresses hang
unused, your skin so thin and translucent,
it wants to flare and rise.

FLASH FLOOD

That summer it didn't stop.
After an inch or two, another
and another for the already bulging earth.
The bridges thrummed with the river's
high current, and for weeks Lincoln's statue
stood in a brown lake, mosquitoes
in thick clouds. The farmers
didn't say "Rain is our life" when
they came in for coffee, glancing
back over their shoulders at the sky.
They said nothing, drank and drummed
the counter with their idle fingers.
And the salesmen who had called me "sweet lips,"
looked past me, or into their catalogs.
Then one night a flash flood carried
cars and bodies into the corn fields.
Bridges lifted from their concrete moorings
and the fields lay submerged under the gray
steam of morning, under the sky
which had unleashed on our helplessness.
It seemed like time itself had opened
its dam, rushing the world toward
its end. And yet, the busses sloshed
their great tires through the streets
and I stood once again on my aching ankles
asking, "May I fill your cup?" and poured
the way that summer poured, the way
the days always pour, our tin cups
full of holes. And still we hold them up.
"Water," we beg. "Something for the next
hour," as it runs past our ears, collects
around our feet, slowly rises, and waits
for us to lie down in it.

THE GARDENS OF THE BODY

1535 in Paris, Vesalius
tells the truth about the body,
labels each glistening part.
Then, in Padua, sets it all down.
Fabrica, he called it, the wondrous
interweaving of nerve, bone and blood.
A garden to be named, each fruit
and flower patterned for itself
and the other.
        I have watched
a surgeon reach into the plum-rich
heart as it pumped, a tiny blade
on his forefinger for the stony valve,
and witnessed the ashen skin grow pink
as dawn. But also, in autopsy,
the skin laid back like lily petals,
vital centers drying. The pathologist
sat beside, eating a sandwich
and listening to the sweet sound
of his pulse.
        I fear my body
crushed or stopped, this fabric scrim
which falls, the way a garden falls,
the way one fleshy pear falls, holding
within it an entire tree, the sucking
roots, the bridal bloom, and the light,
which in Vesalius glowed in a place
he never found.

WILD GRAPES

Grandfather, dying in November,
asked for wild grapes from
a distant creek. He remembered them,
sweet under the leaves, sent Peter,
his eldest, on horseback.
Through the window the light,
golden as broth, filled his bedside cups,
and the dusty air shimmered.

I have known others who, at the end,
crushed the flesh of nectarine against
the dry palate, or swallowed bits
of cake, eyes brimming.

What to drink in remembrance
of each morning that offered itself
with open arms? What food
for the moments we whispered
into its brightness?

Grandfather, the last pain-filled days,
dreamed cures. He who loved God,
who would go to him, but who also
loved this world, filled as it is
with such indescribable beauty,
you have to eat it.

WATERMELON PICKLES

After the sweet sucking
and the spitting of seeds,
our mothers made pickles
of the rinds, like
a second grace.
The watermelon, swollen
with the secrets of summer,
the sugars of long days
traveling the tough,
dusty vine, a slashed paradise
for our mouths and chins.
Then, the boiling of rinds
in the vinegary syrup
for those pale chunks
of astringent amens.
Women in late winter
counting jars in the cellar,
the very old, translucent
at afternoon windows,
calling out our names.

COUNTRY HOME

Doris finds her home,
the one she fled, six years old,
clutching her father's hand.
She walks down the long lane
under the sky from which the bombs fell,
walks into her house
now claimed by a Polish family.

Doris has no place to flee except
on the water, no rescue unless
that water becomes ice. She
and a thousand others run
in terrified breathing toward
the rumor of a ship,
toward a rough lift of the arms
into a whirl of faces on a deck
where wild explosions rock
the face of her mother.

She walks out of her house.
We take her picture with the smiling
family, and another one of the storks
on the rooftip, of their nest
open to the squalls and downpours,
and afterward, the glare of the sun.

FLOODTIDES OF POLAND

Rain glazes the rise of dikes
and the elms that arch the narrow lanes.
The marshy fields swell and throb,
spill into streams toward the Vistula River
in its ribboned shine. It glides
in calm, but fierce necessity, pressing
the packed weight of earth dams,
as it has for centuries. Soft,
green rain on the river, on the reclaimed
fields and muddy dikes, gathering
until it breaks through, until
it lifts barns, crops and tables
in roar and ecstasy. Until it has its way.

*

We drive past the sea of hayfields,
    sun out at last, workers pitching
        into horsedrawn wagons, women my age,
stocky and brown in floral housedresses,
    lifting great forkfuls in repeated arcs.
        They swing the fragrance of stem and seed,
heap for the aching body's hungers.
    They tip the centuries back and forth
        in the shimmering fields which roll on and on
            like waves laboring toward some distant shore.

*

In old Gdansk, street after street
of gabled Dutch houses, but nothing remains
of my family name except an earthen defense
against the flood of invasion. A bastion
named after Adam Wiebe, world's best
water engineer invited from Haarlingen in 1616.
And a medal in the archives for his invention
of the cable system, so carefully calculated
that the filled buckets could move up without power.
Such precision among the tides—the earth
lifted, the flood captured to rise
in the city fountains. A fine tuning,
like the fiddler leaning into the old Dutch
archway. A laborer, sunburned, he scrapes
and presses for the exact tone, loosening it
to float over the medieval weighing station
and up over the green dike, letting it go.

*

What the flood leaves is the lush overgrowth
of neglected cemeteries, Queen Anne's lace
up to my shoulders. And here
a young woman's face, classic,
on a nearly buried stone. She gazes
at the shifting shadow of my footsteps.
Carved cheeks and eyes, testimony
to a short life of greening. Like the amber
on my finger, sap from a pine which fell
six million years ago, present now
in its lamplit glow. And a tiny leaf
in it, caught and saved.

*

Morning mass in St. Nicholas
and the church is rocking.
        It is a ship on the swell
    with ribs of black marble
and gilded railings.
    We are rocking, Nicholas
        of the Sailors,
    in your giant shoe,
and you are scattering pieces of gold
    to save our daughters.
        As your ship lists and sways
    the old women stumble
in the aisle, swinging
    their string bags, Nicholas
        of the great red lap,
    the soft-bearded whispers,
rocking, rocking.

    *

Torun, and in the dusk
of the old city square
the figure of Copernicus
holds the sun in his outstretched hand.
In the stopped bronze moment,
he offers the fiery mass
contained in a cool metal ball,
like a thought, freed
from the spinning orbit of the self,
a place to rest before
the flaring of the night.

SOMETIMES HOPE

The mountainsides blazed
for weeks, ashes falling
on our heads as we stood
in the hazy air.
And then our son came home
with his blackened gear
and slept for days.
He had fought fire with fire
to do the impossible.
Now we see it, the giant
black slash with stumps
in grotesque postures,
acres and acres where nothing
moves or sings, where
nothing waits.

But sometimes hope
is a black ghost
in a fantastic twist,
an old dream that flickers
in the wind.
Not the worried twining
of selfish prayers, but
a reach for something
extravagant, something holy,
like fire itself,
which in its madness
devours the forest for the sky,
and then dreams a new greening,
shoots everywhere breaking
through the crust of ash.

MOCKINGBIRD

Each July morning he reminds us
from the top of the cedar
that all we do is borrow,
borrow and reorder the patterns
and pitches of millenia.
And yet, in this blue
and irretrievable chunk of summer,
he sculpts the air with an order
of sounds which gives light
a new name, for the way it arrives
in bold silks and then
begins its fires in the dust.

He is our *Vorsänger,* the one
who is lining-out for the waking
congregation of Lane Avenue.
"The one who must breathe the text,"
Alice Parker insists, and begins,
"When all thy mercies, O my God . . . "
And we follow, one by one,
lifting our rib cages with our borrowed breath,
and rise into another day—pure gift—
as it balances on the tip
of the highest branch.

WALNUT ORCHARD

Complete shade under leaf
upon leaf, like hand upon hand.

It is a summer weight
that sunlight can't penetrate.

A deep, redolent darkness
between the damp soil and a thousand

extended arms. This
is where we walk, then stop,

holding our memories like books
with layered pages of a loneliness

we love. No sound, no need
for sound, our ears turning

toward a time when longing loosens
and falls, leaf by rasping leaf.

WHITE FIELD

After your death I think *black rose,*
but write *white field,* the way you would,
a light in your eyes. The field near my house,
feathery with wild oats and blowing in May.
I write *field under full moon,* dry,
like a cough or hair bleached and falling,
what you left us, plow's blade cutting in
and the air filled with dust. It's rootedness
that lies exposed and flies. It's old
mother earth, her suck and murmurings
lifted with a groan and given up.
Not the elegance I try to shape
from her rough roots. It's these shifting,
blowing lines, you in the air I breathe.

for Ernesto Trejo (1950-1991)

IN NOVEMBER

The trees are dropping
their fiery tongues.
Under spread limbs
the hushed piles lie,
waiting to be found.
Gingko, ash and liquid amber
stand over their last
annunciations and listen,
the way the walls in a room
listen, and the wood of chairs
listens, and this table
where I sit.

"The doors have ears,"
my father used to say
to stop family gossip.
"But doors can't tell,"
I thought, shutting them
against the draft.
But now when I awaken
and smell smoke, I sniff
every dim room for what
is true—the utterance
of the wood cell's slow burn,
a hummed syllable of emptying.

PHOTOGRAPHS OF THE WILD

As a child in the parlors of the old,
I saw Victorian women posed in front of waterfalls
and the great redwoods, 3-D through the stereopticon.
Now I stand before the same trees, smiling
with my children before they run along the rough
bark of the fallen giants. The camera fixes
our gaze, but we move on, packing up once more.
Even in those moth ball-scented rooms
the old women stroked my hair and disappeared,
the roar in the pictures having called them away.

*

Snapshots of our green '54 Ford
in the tunneled heart of the Wawona Tree,
the children on the stump of the giant
Centennial, a slice for Philadelphia
where they called it a hoax, missing
the point. The way we mostly do,
except the child looking.
It's like the whole universe,
our small daughter cries out, stretching her arms.
Love is like this, I once wrote.
Not the rose. Two thousand years they stand,
fire-gutted they stand, with enormous clawed feet,
grasping the loose loam of this earth.

*

The blonde hills stretch for miles,
nude women reclining, or a pride of lions
under the sky's ceramic blue.
All is ease, even in the shadowed folds.
All hunger satiated, no head raised
to test the wind. And yet, under the dreaming
skins, grassroots stir and the blades
shiver with stories from the sea.
Some who enter are lost.

*

We take pictures of the children scrambling
rocks at Lover's Point where the Methodists
once strolled and prayed to Jesus, the wild one.
Be daring, leave home, he called out.
But also, be like a planted vine.
Among the turmoil, the settled heart.
Would you rather drown or burn, my small son asks,
safe in bed. I stroke his arm as he drowses
in this valley between the roar and the silent,
scorched hills. As he descends night's ladder.
Drown, I think. Giving myself back in full weight.
And yet, that lightness of ash, the photo
going up in a flare.

*

Profiled figure on the mountain cliff's overhang,
one silhouette looking out to sea.
Emily in her one portrait and seventeen hundred poems.
"Wild nights, wild nights, were I with thee . . ."
That longing to moor the self to love's chaos.
I lift her words like a glass to the call
of this earth. I drink to the waterfalls
and the wilderness snows that feed the vine,
and to its fruit, the crushed worlds of sugar and light.

BLUE PIANO

(painting by Peter Janzen)

The piano waits
holding its pool
of gold, waits

for the blue hammers
to beat at the forge.
Chords, the repeated note,

runs and cadenzas
beating, vibrating,
sparks flying off

shaping the air
into something whole,
all the tones

melding into curve
and movement—
something I can ride.

I will gallop into
the dark,
horseshoes flashing.

ABOUT THE POET

Jean Wiebe Janzen was born in Saskatchewan, Canada, raised in the midwestern United States, and now lives in Fresno, California. She completed her undergraduate studies at Fresno Pacific College and received the master of arts at California State University of Fresno. She has won a fellowship from the National Endowment for the Arts, and other awards. Her previous books are *Words for the Silence* (1984), *Three Mennonite Poets* (1986), and *The Upside-Down Tree* (1992). She teaches poetry writing at Fresno Pacific College, in the Fresno area public schools, and at Eastern Mennonite University in Virginia. Her husband, Louis Janzen, and she have four children and six grandchildren.